Sewing

Absolute Beginner's Guide to Sewing

with Speed, Creativity, and Mastery

Mary Keaton

paraphrase any part or the content within this book without the consent of the author or copyright owner. Legal action will be pursued if this is breached.

<u>Disclaimer Notice:</u>

Please note the information contained within this document is for educational and entertainment purposes only. Every attempt has been made to provide accurate, up to date and reliable complete information. No warranties of any kind are expressed or implied. Readers acknowledge that the author is not engaging in the rendering of legal, financial, medical or professional advice.

By reading this document, the reader agrees that under no circumstances are we responsible for any losses, direct or indirect, which are incurred as a result of the use of information contained within this document, including, but not limited to, —errors, omissions, or inaccuracies.

Table of Contents

Introduction

Sewing used to be a daily task for some people but with the advent of cheap, bulk-produced clothing, people stopped sewing their own clothes and household items. Happily, interest has picked up again and more and more people are picking up their needles again. With craft stores everywhere and sewing machines available in shops on every corner, the DIY culture is back with a vengeance. Instead of blank or sneering looks, now when you make your own clothes you'll find people asking you how you do it and if you can show them.

I wrote this book with the complete beginner in mind. I have split it into sections, covering hand sewing and machine sewing before moving on to a few simple projects for you to try. I will tell you about the equipment you need, how to get started, and some of the basic stitches in both machine and hand sewing.

I will also give you some of the more advanced techniques to learn. These are techniques that any sewer, no matter what their level of experience is, should add to their repertoire. It is these techniques that will give your garments and other items a professional finished look, with pockets, zippers, and other decorative embellishments and stitches.

I have tried to make things easy to understand with step-by-step directions where needed. This book is written assuming you have absolutely no knowledge of sewing whatsoever. I don't expect you to understand everything straight away – even the most experienced of sewers took a long time to learn their craft. What I will say is this: sewing is what you make of it. It can be easy or it can be complicated. But with the right amount of concentration and diligence, it really won't take long for you to be able to produce something quite lovely. It doesn't have to be perfect but it will be yours.

In the later part of the book, I have introduced you to the use of blanket stitch, as this is a very decorative element that can be used for various projects. I have also given you a couple of these projects to try out for yourself.

Since sewing is a practical skill, there's no time like the present to mend and alter all those items of clothing that have been lying in your closet for so long. Lean how to take in an item when you have lost weight. Learn how to change the length of a hem on a pre-bought dress. In fact, all kinds of repairs are covered in this book.

I have also taken the opportunity to teach you to use sewing patterns, as this opens up all kinds of possibilities. You will be able to create clothing based on really good, quality patterns made for beginners. This means your work will be less hit and miss and that you will get great results every time. Don't be baffled by all the markings on a pattern. I show you how to use and understand them because that's half the battle.

Keep on practicing and you will soon be turning out dresses, skirts, and bags while you watch your favorite TV show! So dive in, have a go, and take things at your own pace. Only you can decide what you can do and what challenges you are prepared to face and win. Only you can decide whether to make an occasional item or an entire wardrobe!

The Origin of Sewing

Sewing is the art of using a needle and thread to attach pieces of shaped material together to create a piece of clothing, a bag, tea towels, placemats, curtains and so on. It really is nothing new to the human race and can actually be dated back as far back as the prehistoric era. Some archeologists believe that, in the last Ice Age, almost 25,000 years ago, needle and thread were used to sew furs, hides, bark, and skins together to produce clothing. Indeed, prehistoric needles have been discovered, made from ivory, animal bones, and antlers. Needles made from wood and other natural materials from the Agave plant have been recorded as being used by various Native American tribes.

The oldest iron sewing needle can be dated back to the 3rd century BC and came from Germany, the Celtic Hill Fort at Manching. Chinese archaeologists have reported finds of thimbles and an entire set of needles, found in the tomb of a Han Dynasty official that date to 202 BC. So far, this is the oldest recorded thimble ever found and would have been used to push the needles through barks and animal skins, or any material that was tough or highly resistant. The first thimbles were constructed from wood, bark, and bone. Later versions were made from porcelain, leather, and glass. Eventually, the thimble became a type of ornament when people started to put metals and precious stones on them.

The sewing thread was originally made out of catgut, sinew, veins, and plant fibers, just as a single strand thread. It didn't take long to realize that these animal and plant fibers could be spun together to produce stronger multiple strand thread. Egyptians used to spin plant fibers, hair, and wool from animals to produce strong threads. Together with the Phoenicians, the Egyptians developed ways of coloring these threads, using dyes made from plants, berries, and other ingredients. Later on, the Japanese and the Chinese came up with a process of using silkworm cocoons to spin silk threads.

For many thousands of years, all sewing was done by hand. When the sewing machine was invented, it revolutionized the sewing industry, making it easy for people to stitch up a garment in just a matter of minutes. Karl Wiesenthal, a German inventor, invented the first sewing machine with a needle in 1755. Unfortunately, he did not get the credit because he never completed the machine. In 1790, a British inventor by the name of Thomas Saint completed a working sewing machine and promptly patented it. However, he never rose to fame because the machine never went beyond the model he built for his patent.

It would 40 years before a practical machine was invented and patented in 1930 by a French tailor called Barthelemy Thirmonnier. This was the start of the sewing machine era. In the years that followed, different models and variations were produced and patents were registered in an era that took the sewing industry by storm. Despite that, hand sewing was still very widely used and, while it began with the creation of clothing, it soon extended to shoes, sporting goods, bookbinding, upholstery, and sail making. Today, many of these are still produced with hand sewing while machines still produce clothing and other items in bulk.

It is worth noting that sewing has taken on many guises over the years. Although you may associate it with dressmaking, it has also been used for decorative elements, such as making family crests or embroidery pictures. Even in this day and age, the variety of projects you can try once you learn to sew is amazing and very diverse indeed.

You will learn how to use stitches to decorate items yourself from this book following in the rich history of your ancestors.

Part 1 – Hand Sewing

Have you ever started to cook a fabulous recipe but found halfway through you don't have everything you need to complete it? Using substitutes doesn't always work and the dish just doesn't taste or look like it should. The same goes for completing a successful sewing project - if you don't have the right tools on hand, you just can't do it.

As I said at the start, this book is written with complete beginners in mind so, starting from scratch, I would imagine your first shopping trip to find those tools would go something like this:

- You go to your favorite store and head for the sewing section

- You stand there, looking around, dazed at the sheer amount of choice – sewing tools, gadgets, materials, threads, needles, and all those different sewing machines

- You walk out, somewhat intimidated and very confused

The Hand Sewing Kit

Have you ever seen one of those little travel kits for sewing? It contains a pair of tiny scissors, a few threads in different colors, a few needles and pins, maybe even a plastic thimble. Now think on a larger scale and you have the basic hand sewing kit, along with a few extras, of course. I am going to give you a list of all the tools you need to begin your hand-sewing journey – take this list to the store with you and I guarantee you will come away with everything you need.

- Straight pins

- Hand sewing needles

- A needle threader

- A pair of shears

- A seam ripper

- A tape measure

- A seam gauge

- A clear gridded ruler

- Fabric marker pens and pencils

- Thread

- Thimble

Now let's look at this list in more detail.

Straight Pins

Proper dressmaker or all-purpose pins are made out of stainless steel, rust proofed and ideal for pinning most of the fabrics that you would use. You can get flat-headed pins or pins with glass or plastic rounded heads. Most sewers tend to choose round headed pins, partly because they are easier to see and easier to grab hold of. If you do use pins on a regular basis, it may be a good idea to buy yourself a pincushion. This is a quick place to put pins during the course of your work and it a very handy gadget to have.

Hand Sewing Needles

There are loads of different needles available and all for different purposes. Don't waste a lot of time on these because you will be a little bamboozled by all the different types and sizes. Simply purchase an assortment of different ones or buy a package that contains a range of sizes and types. You will find you are more comfortable with certain needles anyway and you will tend to stick with them, no matter what you are sewing. A little common sense is all that is needed here – don't use a heavy thick needle for sewing materials that are light and delicate and don't use a light skinny needle for sewing heavy fabrics like denim. You will also find needles are divided into what are called Sharp and Crewel types. These are used for different elements of sewing, such as embroidery and basting. Have a variety on hand because different needles will suit different tasks and a good set of needles is usually available at a very reasonable price.

Needle Threader

Threading a needle is not always easy – trying to get that bit of thread through a tiny little eye! Even the experts use needle threaders because they make the job so much easier so do make sure you get one. A needle threader is a small metal gadget that has a wire loop on it. The loop goes through the eye of the needle, the thread goes through the wire loop and then you pull it back through the eye. The loop is rigid, so it is easier to get it through the needle than trying to push a bit of thread through. These are particularly handy if you have problems with your eyes.

Shears

There are lots of different kinds of cutting tools but the best ones are a simple pair of shears. The difference between shears and scissors is that the shears have different sized handles, whereas scissors are the same size. These different handles give you better leverage and, because the handles are also slightly bent upwards, the fabric can stay flat while you are cutting it. Think about buying one pair for fabric and one for paper – when you cut paper it can dull the blades and you don't want to be cutting material with blunt blades. Pinking shears are another thing altogether. These are used to cut in a zigzag fashion so that you don't have to finish off the seams. These may be useful for work with certain fabrics that do not fray and when you want a neat finish on the inside.

Seam Ripper

This is an essential part of your kit because no one person is perfect and we all make mistakes. There will be times when you need to rip open a seam and start again. This tool makes it easy. It is a small tool, about pencil-width, with a small, pronged blade. All you do is slide the blade along the seam and gently tug – the stitches will cut through but the fabric won't be damaged.

Tape Measure

Buy a flexible tape measure, not a rigid one and make sure it is 60 inches in length. Most are. You should have one with imperial units on one side and metric on the other. Do keep in mind the fabric tape measures will stretch over time so you will need to replace it every so often. Keep it neatly put away in your sewing box, as many a seamstress has been angered by not being able to find it when it is needed. Sewing tape measures actually roll up into a neat coil and can have a neat place in your sewing box.

Seam Gauge

A seam gauge is a small plastic or metal ruler, 6 inches in length, and a sliding gauge that goes along the whole ruler. These little tools make the job of constantly measuring seam allowances and hems easy and can also help to mark out topstitching. Bear in mind your machine will also have a guide for seams, so learn to use them when you are using your machine, as it will make your life easier.

Clear Gridded Ruler

These are about 18 inches long and 2 inches wide and are marked with inches, half-inches, quarter, and eighth-inches on a grid. The reason for getting a clear one is obvious – when you put it on your fabric, you can see it through it. This is another tool you will need to replace regularly because plastic marks easily and can become opaque with age.

Fabric Pens and Pencils

Transferring a pattern to fabric is easy with the right tools. You should buy special fabric marking pens and pencils. Normal writing tools are not advisable because the ink or lead marks may not wash out of the fabric. The fabric markers are designed so they do wash out. These may be labeled as "tailor's chalk" in some shops.

Thread

The single most important thing, when you buy thread, is to go for quality. The best and most common is polyester-wrapped cotton, which can be used for just about any type of sewing you want to do. Do not buy cheap threads, as the chances are they will break and the cotton won't be even and smooth. When you pick up a thread spool check that it has a smooth finish and isn't fuzzy. It's a good idea to have black and white thread at all times, as these are the most commonly used threads, but having a cross section of colors in your workbox will help you when you are faced with small jobs. The color used for jeans is also a common thread you will use a lot; so make sure you have this in stock.

Thimbles

I have no doubt you saw your grandmother or mother using one of these. The job of a thimble is to protect your fingertip when you push the needle through the material – even the blunt end of a needle can hurt! Most sewers don't tend to use a thimble unless they are sewing heavy fabrics but get one and try it and see how you get on. When you are mending jeans, believe me, you will be thankful you bought one!

How to use a thimble

If you have never used one before, you might be surprised to learn that there is a technique to using a thimble.

- Choose a thimble that is comfortable on the middle finger of the hand you are going to be using for sewing

- Place it on that middle finger – left if you are left-handed and right if you are right-handed.

- Grasp the needle firmly between your index finger and thumb

- Push the needle into the material and then use the end or the side of the thimble to push it through the material

Threading a needle

For the Eagle-Eyed

- Choose the needle that suits you and/or the project you are sewing

- Choose the right thread

- Reel about 18 to 24 inches off the spool and, using a sharp pair of scissors, cut the thread off the spool at an angle of 45 degrees

- Push the cut end through the needle eye – you might find it easier to damp the end of the thread before you do this

- Pull the thread about 4 or 5 inches through the needle – this end will not have a knot in it

For the not so eagle-eyed

- Use a needle threader

- Push the metal loop through the needle eye

- Hold the threaded the needle in one hand and push the thread through the loop with the other hand – push through about 4 or 5 inches

- Pull the threader gently back through the eye

You can also purchase self-threading needles that have a slot. Sometimes this slot will be beside and sometimes it will be on top of the needle eye. Slide the thread gently into the notch beside the slot until it catches and then you just snap the thread into the needle eye.

Helpful tips

- Have plenty of light – if natural light is an issue, have a good lamp positioned over you so you can see what you are doing.

- Use a little beeswax on the end of the thread to stiffen it up and help it push through the eye. Alternatively, you can lick the thread.

- Put a piece of paper or card behind the needle. Use a contrasting color to the thread you're using so it is easier to see. For example, if you are threading white cotton, use a dark colored piece of card or paper and vice versa. I tend to hold the needle toward the light so I can clearly see the eye.

Tying the knot

It is very easy to tie a knot, as you most likely know, but there is a specific way to do it when you are sewing. Practice until you get a feel for it.

- Hold the thread firmly between your index finger and thumb

- Loop the thread around the tip of your index finger on your other hand, wrapping it just at the bottom of your nail

- Close your thumb down over the loop

- Holding the thread as taut as you can, use your thumb to roll the thread's loop towards the tip of your index finger

- As it slides off your index finger, use your middle finger to hold the loop while you pull the thread into a knot

Until you get accustomed to sewing, it's likely you will use a knot to anchor the thread when you start new work. However, with time, you will learn to do a double stitch on the back of the work so the thread is anchored and there is no need for a knot.

Type of Hand Stitches

I am going to talk about seven of the most common types of hand stitches you can use. There are many, many more but these should be sufficient for you to start learning and to complete most hand-sewn projects.

To start, thread your needle and tie the knot, as per the above instructions.

Basting Stitch

This stitch is used to hold pieces together temporarily – usually if you are doing some machine sewing and need to stop pieces from shifting. And yes, you can use a machine to create a basting stitch, but it is far better done by hand.

- Create a dashed line look by weaving the needle in and out of the fabric

- Place the stiches between ¼ and ½ inch apart, leaving equal spaces between each one

- Do not lock the stitch, either at the beginning or at the end

Running Stitch

This is similar to the basting stitch but we use smaller stitches and we also use a locking stitch at the end. You can also use a lock stitch at the beginning if you like. The stitches should be short, about ⅛ inch in length, and spaced out evenly. Of course, this is a guide, and the size of the stitch will depend on what fabric you are using. Lightweight fabric requires small stitches while the heavyweights need a wider stitch.

The running stitch is the hand sewer's version of the sewing machine stitch. While the sewing machine has precision and tightness, the hand stitch is easier for fixing seams that are starting to come apart. It is also a good stitch to use in spaces the machine can't get to, or when you are sewing very small seams. This is the original stitch, the one that was used to hold material together before the sewing machine was invented.

Backstitch

The backstitch is used to create strong seams and is often used on heavyweight fabrics or as a way of repairing a torn seam. With the backstitch, you work from right to left, starting at the right side of the opening.

- Take the needle up through the fabric

- Pull it through and go down through the fabric again to create a single stitch

- Now bring the needle up through the fabric again, a little space off from the first stitch

- Insert the needle and push it backwards through the hole created by the last stitch

- Repeat until you have covered the entire area

Backstitch is used to replace machine stitching and can be used for small repairs if you don't want to get the machine out to do them.

Overcast Stitch

This is sometimes known as the whipstitch and is used to finish off edges that have been cut to stop them from unraveling. This stitch is helpful for materials like linens and gabardines that are prone to fraying. You can also use this stitch to mend a tear:

- Bring your needle up on one side of the edge you are finishing

- Create a number of even diagonal stitches that loop over the fabric edge

- What you are doing will depend on how close you keep the stitches together – mending stitches, for example, would be very close together, almost on top of one another

Step or Ladder Stitch

Also known as the slipstitch, this is one of the most useful of all the hand stitches. Slipstitches are used to make an invisible seam between folded edges or between a folded and a flat edge. You can also use them for bindings, to finish off the seam on a pillow, to apply applique, or to close linings.

- Iron the folds, making sure they are flat

- Start by slipping the needle through the inside of the fold so the knot is hidden

- Bring it up through the folded edge and put it down through the opposite fold, directly across

- Slide the needle along the edge, about ⅛ inch to ¼ inch, and push the needle back out

- Pull the thread straight up and then insert the needle directly across in the opposite fold

- Continue this until the opening you are sewing is closed

You will see where the name "ladder" stitch comes from, as you have created what looks like a ladder. Keep your stitches smooth and tight and try to match the thread to your fabric to create almost invisible stitches.

Blind Hem Stitch

Just like the ladder stitch, the idea here is to pick up just a little bit of fabric with each of the stitches and, using a matching thread, you should be able to minimize how much of the stitching shows.

- Slip the needle under the fold so the knot is hidden

- Bring it out through the folded hem edge

- Pick up a few threads of fabric with the point of your needle and take this from the flat fabric where the hem is sitting

- Bring the needle into the folded edge and repeat all the way around the hem

Securing Stitch

No matter which type of stitch you are using, you must finish it off with a securing stitch, otherwise it will all come undone. The only exception to this is the basting stitch.

- Make a small backstitch and loop the thread over the needle point

- Pull the thread through to make a knot at the base of the fabric

- Repeat two or three times if you want a stronger lock

That completes this tutorial on the basics of hand sewing. Next we move on to the sewing machine.

Part 2 – Machine Sewing

Obviously, to begin this, you will need a sewing machine. Most machines come with a set of tools but do check, because you will need the following:

- Sewing machine

- Sewing machine needles

- Bobbins

- Presser foot

- Zipper foot

- Small screwdriver

- Sewing machine oil

- Small brush

Let's look at these in closer detail.

Sewing Machine

For a beginner, the most basic sewing machine you can find is the best way to start, so don't let the store talk you into buying an all-singing, all-dancing model that does a thousand different stitches! You don't need it at this stage and a basic model is relatively inexpensive. While you are looking for a sewing machine, look at all the details. Look at the cards and the booklets that come with the machines and ask to test as many as it takes to know which one is right for you. You may not be paying a fortune for it but you still need a sewing machine you are comfortable with.

Things to Consider

Take some time to think about what you will be using your sewing machine for. Is it for making clothes or curtains? Are you just going to be using it for simple projects and mending? Or are you thinking about using it for quilting or something else later on? All you need is a simple mechanical sewing machine, one that does both straight and zigzag stitching. Later on, when you are happy with the machine, you can always upgrade. Try to establish what your needs are before you purchase a machine. Don't buy one just because it has a lot of gadgets because you may not ever get around to using them. Perhaps you could try one that has a simple buttonhole facility because this is relatively easy to learn. Having different lengths of stitches is certainly advantageous when choosing a machine.

Choosing the Right Machine

Think about how often your sewing machine is going to be used. There isn't any point in purchasing an expensive complicated sewing machine with all the bells and whistles on it if you are only going to use it sporadically. On the other hand, if you are going to be doing regular sewing work with it, then you will need one with plenty of different stitches on it and all the add-ons that will save you time, like a one-step button hole feature and the quick-drop bobbin case.

You must also consider what you need from the machine in terms of what you are going to be making. For example, a person who makes clothes and curtains will want a sewing machine that is very different from one who is only using it for machine embroidery. The best thing to do is to write a list of everything you want to do with your new machine and all the features you want it to have before you start your search. Speak to other people who own a sewing machine. Their feedback is vital to you because they can talk you through various features of a machine and maybe come up with ideas for features you hadn't thought of. They can also give you some advice on brands or types of machine to stay away from, or those they particularly like.

Types of Sewing Machines

Mechanical

Mechanical sewing machines require no electricity source to work and are the most basic of all machines. However, because there is no electrical help, you do need to use a fair bit of muscle power, as you will need to operate a dial or wheel on the side of the machine to make the needle and bobbin work. These days, there aren't too many mechanical machines made and those you do find will mostly be vintage, like the well-known black Singer sewing machine. However, in spite of the fact they are very basic and have little in the way of mod cons, they are great machines for basic projects and will go through most types of material, although they are best for light to medium fabric. People who undertake only light projects typically use mechanical sewing machines.

Electronic

As the name suggests, these sewing machines run off an electric motor that powers up the lights on the sewing machine (if it has any), the bobbin, and the needle. These are operated by way of a foot pedal. Similar to driving a vehicle, the more pressure you apply on the foot pedal, the faster you will sew. To do a reverse stitch on these sewing machines, there is a designated lever you will find on the main body of the machine. These are good all-rounders and are suitable for a whole range of sewing projects because they feature a wide range of stitches. You can also alter the stitch length and the tension so you can use a lot of different threads and materials.

Computerized

The experienced machinist generally uses the computerized sewing machine. They are packed full of features, including a ton of different stitch functions and good range of ways in which they can be altered to fit the needs of the machinist. Instead of having a selection dial to pick the stitch you want to use, there is a key or touchpad that has to be pressed. You will then see the stitch image or the stitch number on a screen. On some of the more complex computerized sewing machines, you can even upload patterns you have downloaded from the Internet and, on some; you have the option of designing your own patterns and stitches.

Computerized sewing machines are more expensive than both the electronic and mechanical models. They are best suited to the professional machinist who will make use of the machine on a daily basis to make items for selling.

Overlockers

Overlockers are a kind of machine used for finishing off and are usually used by sewers who make clothes and craft items for sale. The machine gives these items a professional, neat finish, as they are able to sew a seam, finish off the edges, and trim off any excess fabric all in one hit. These are good for the simple project that needs no extras, like buttonholes or zippers, as an overlocker does not have the functions to do this. One word of advice – if you do buy one of these, have a trial run before you overlock the final piece because they handle in a very different way to a normal sewing machine and you will need some practice!

Sewing Machine Needles

Like needles used when hand-sewing, you are better off buying a selection of different ones, or variety packs. Most packages of sewing machine needles contain a range, usually a couple of each size. What you will find is sewing machine needles are usually color-coded and have a number. The rule of thumb here is the lower numbers are smaller needles while the higher ones denote the bigger needles. Most projects can be taken care of with a size 10 to 12 needle but if you are using heavy fabrics, you will need a higher number. Keep in mind; lower numbered needles are best for lightweight fabrics.

When choosing needles, do read your sewing machine manual, as there will be guidelines for your particular model.

Bobbins

The sewing machine uses two threads; an upper and a lower thread that lock together to form a strong stitch. The upper thread comes from the spool on the spindle on top of the machine and the lower thread comes from the bobbin. The bobbin is like a mini version of the spool inside the machine. Most machines will have a couple of spares in the box. You can never have too many of these, though, so get a few more spares to be on the safe side. It will save you a lot of time having to unwind the bobbin whenever you need a new color of thread. I tend to use my machine for a variety of jobs, but always keep a bobbin ready of white and black for instant access for standard jobs.

Presser Foot

Whichever type of machine you buy, it will come with a basic presser foot. This is what holds the material down while the machine sews it. The presser foot is important because it keeps the fabric stable, which allows you to make sure you are sewing an even, straight line. The standard foot will have a prong that sits flat on both sides of the needle. It doesn't hurt to have a spare to hand.

Zipper Foot

While you are at it, get a zipper foot. While you might not be planning to put any zips in just yet, it doesn't hurt to have one – just in case. Instead of the two prongs, the zipper foot has just one. This is what allows the needle to get right up to the zip teeth while the material is still held in place. Zipper feet can also be used to put piping and cording on home décor items.

Small Screwdriver

Have a small flathead screwdriver to hand, because you will need it to loosen off and tighten up the screw that holds the needle in place. Without the screwdriver, you can't change the needle. It will also help you to get into areas that need oiling. Usually, machines come with a small toolbox of tools and you would be wise to keep these somewhere safe so you have them on hand when you need them.

Small Brush

A small bristle brush is ideal for cleaning your sewing machine. As you use your machine, it will collect lint, dust, and tiny bits of thread. If you don't clean it out regularly, it will start to slow down or jam up. Pay attention to brushing out underneath the presser foot, the bobbin area, and any other little space where dirt and dust can get in. It doesn't have to be anything special; a small paintbrush with firm bristles will do the job.

You will find that the area that gets clogged up the most is where the bobbin goes. This may get dust and bits of fabric caught in it and I make a point of cleaning this area between each use so there is not a build-up felting that stops the machine working to its maximum effect.

How to Set Up a Sewing Machine

Whether this is your very first time using a sewing machine or you need a refresher, this next section is going to walk you through how to set up your machine.

Step 1 – Plug it in

Plug in the cable to your machine and then to the power socket. Position the pedal where you can comfortably reach it on the floor. Don't turn the machine on at this stage, otherwise you might find yourself in a bit of pain!

Step 2 - Attach the needle

In some machines, the needle is already in place, but in others, you will need to attach it. If it is already in place, you still need to know how to change it if it breaks or if you need to use a different sized needle for your project. In some cases, the needle will go blunt and you will need a new sharp one.

To take the needle out, twist the knob a couple of times that is to the right of the needle in order to loosen it. Pull it out. To put a new one in, push it up into the hole and tighten up the knob again. The needle has a rounded top on the front and flat at the back so you will know which way it has to go in.

Step 3 – Attach the presser foot

This is what holds down the fabric and helps guide the needle. You can get all sorts of different feet for different stiches but, at this stage, we'll just worry about the standard foot. The presser foot is located behind the needle on the end of the bar. You can see there is a lever to the right that allows you to raise and lower the foot as needed.

Some machines have feet that snap on while others are held in with screws. However, if it is held on, raise the bar with the lever, put the foot underneath, and lower the bar. Either it will click into place or you will need to tighten it with screws. To raise it ready for use, lift the lever again. To take the foot off, flick the lever you will find at the back of the bar and the foot will drop, or loosen the screws if yours is manual.

How to Thread a Sewing Machine

Once you know how to do it, it's a quick and easy process to thread your sewing machine. Practice really does make perfect, so keep on trying and you will get to the stage where you can thread your machine in seconds.

Step 1 – Wind the bobbin

As I said earlier, the sewing machine uses two threads: the reel at the top and the bobbin from down below. The bobbins are always supplied empty and the reels are bought fully wound. Before you can thread the machine, the first thing to do is get the thread off the reel and onto the bobbin.

Put the reel of thread onto the spool pin at the top of the machine – you can't miss it; it's the prong that sticks out from the machine. Some are top spool pins while other machines have pins that go out to the left and have a cover on them to keep the reel in place. The thread should come out from the back towards the left. Unwind a few inches of the thread, pull it left, and wrap it around the front of a little nub that comes out of the top of the machine. Thread some of it up through the little hole in the top of the bobbin and then wrap it a few times around so it comes out of the back and to the left. Put the bobbin onto the bobbin winder and flick it right so it is secured in place.

Some machines allow you pull the hand wheel out to wind the bobbin without moving the needle. If yours is one of these, switch on your sewing machine. Grab the thread that sticks out of the bobbin and press down on the pedal so the thread starts winding off the spool and onto the bobbin. Once it starts winding let go of the thread. If the thread goes onto the winder and not the bobbin, you will need to change the direction the thread is wrapped. Keep on going until the bobbin has as much thread on it as you need and then snip the thread. Flick the winder to the left and turn off your machine; otherwise, you might end up sewing your hand with the next bit!

Step 2 – Thread the spool

The next step is to thread the sewing machine. Start with the thread from the spool at the top and then move on to threading the bobbin.

Check the spool thread is coming out from behind the spool to the left. Guide the thread down to the machine needle – some machines do have arrows that guide you so you can't go wrong. Pull the thread around the first hook to the left, down through the first ditch, up to the left through the second ditch, round hook number two, and down to the second ditch again.

Secure the thread behind the hooks – one is at the front of the sewing machine and the other is beside the needle. Thread through the front of the needle, but snip the thread first so you have a clean end with which to work. If the needle is in the ditch, turn the hand wheel or knob at the side to raise it so you can thread it.

Step 3 – Thread the bobbin

This thread goes into the bottom of the sewing machine. On some sewing machines, the bobbin is located under the needle – there will be a little plastic lid you flip off and put the bobbin in. Some are front-loaded; so you will need to take the arm on the front of the machine off and flip the cover down to see the bobbin holder.

Take the case out. It will be a silver bit in the middle. Put the bobbin of thread in this; pull off a few inches of thread, taking it down into the slit and out the side, then put the case back into the machine.

The next step is to get the bobbin thread to the machine surface. Use the spool thread at the top to do this. Hold the spool thread in your left hand and, with your right hand, turn the wheel one rotation so the needle moves down and then up again. Tug on the top thread gently with your left hand and you should see a loop of the bobbin thread appear at the surface. Loop it with a pen or something similar to pull it out, close the cover and replace the arm on your machine or shut the plastic cover, depending on where your bobbin holder is located.

Some machines these days have a threading mechanism that makes it very simple to thread the machine. Follow the instructions you get with your sewing machine, as each will have its own peculiarities.

Machine Stitches

There is a good chance your sewing machine has one or two tricks hidden away, stitches that you just wouldn't think to use most of the time. Whether you are new to your sewing machine or you've finally just gotten the hang of it and are taking it for granted, maybe now is time to look at what your machine can actually do.

Basic Stitches

Your machine might offer up all or just some of the basic stitches listed below. Compare these with what your machine has, or, if you are going to buy one, make sure you get one that has all of the basics and more besides.

- **Straight stitch** - used for seaming, basting and topstitching.

- **Zigzag stitch** - the sewing machine will add some width to a straight stitch to produce the zigzag stitch. You use this for making buttonholes, stitching around an applique, sewing buttons on and for embroidery. This is a practical stitch and a fun one at the same time. If you produce zigzag stitches that are close together, i.e., a very short length of stitch, it is known as a satin stitch and is used for applique work.

  Keep in mind; zigzag stitches tend to stretch more than a straight stitch does so they are highly useful on elasticated or other stretchy materials. You can use a zigzag stitch if you don't have a serger to finish off your seams. You can also use this stitch on buttonholes as I said earlier but most machines will have a special buttonhole stitch.

- **Three-step zigzag stitch** – When you use the zigzag stitch on its widest width, it will pull the material into a funnel, allowing the material to roll underneath the stitch, which is not the most desirable outcome. To stop this from happening, we get the three-step zigzag stitch. How this works is the needle taking three stitches over to one side and then another three over to the other side. This keeps the fabric flat and stops it from rolling into a funnel shape. You can use this stitch to finish off raw edges, mending tears, sewing on elastic, and for adding decorative touches.

- **Blind hem/stretch blind hemstitch** – the blind hemstitch has been designed to help with hemming woven fabrics. This makes the stitches all but invisible when you look at the garment from the right side. The stretch blind hemstitch adds on an extra couple of zigzag stitches that will stretch so that you can hem knitted fabrics with an invisible stitch. Both of these stitches can be used for adding decorative touches as well.

- **Overlock** – Most overlock features on sewing machines today are designed so they will stitch and finish a seam in one go. This simulates the serger stitch commonly seen on garments that are ready-to-wear. Some of these stitches will work best on knitted fabrics and others on woven fabrics.

- **Decorative stitches** – These fall into two categories: closed satin-like stitches, like the diamond stitch and the ball stitch; and open, tracery-like stitches, like the honeycomb stitch and the daisy stitch. Most of the newer sewing machines can be programmed to combine both of these types of stitch with other stitches in order to elongate a design. This combination gives a bold, decorative look and even allows you to be able to stitch a name.

- **Buttonhole stitch** – as the name suggests, this is used for creating buttonholes. It works by creating a bar tack at either end of two very close together zigzag stitches. When the buttonhole is finished, you can, very carefully, rip the hole open using a proper seam ripper. You might find your machine comes with a special buttonhole foot or a whole host of different attachments that help you to create loads of different types of buttonholes for all different applications.

- **Overcast stitch** – the overcast stitch is used for finishing off raw edges and can be used in place of a serger or a zigzag stitch to finish off a seam. The overcast is not so good as a serger but is better than the zigzag stitch, and you may need to use a special foot for it.

Your particular machine may feature more than 20 different stitches but the ones listed above are the ones you will make the most use of. Most sewing machines, regardless of their type, will come with a range of decorative stitches and special stitches, like the blind hem and stretch stitches.

To get the hang of what you have, get some cheap woven and knit fabrics, sharp needles and play around to learn what your machine can and can't do and how to use it. Don't go full steam ahead; just take it slowly. Have a go at sewing seams, at using all the different types of stitches, and at buttonholes. Learn how and when to adjust tension on certain stitches to keep the top and bottom threads balanced. Learn as much as you can and practice as much as you can before you go "live" on a real piece of work. If you have one of the newest, highest-end sewing machines, you may find you can also create a number of intricate embroidery designs with the use of embroidery cards. These are special computer discs that are able to store a number of large motifs, including intricate and complex ones.

You Are Ready to Sew!

However, before you start actually sewing, it wouldn't be such a bad thing to pull out your thread and have a few practice tries at threading your machine. I know you are eager to get on but this is an important step. Taking the time to learn it now will save you time later on.

Ready? Then let's get sewing! If this is your first time with a machine, it will be somewhat daunting in the beginning. The best advice I can give you is to relax and have a lot of fun. You are not going to be turning out professional looking garments the first time, so grab some old bits of material, something cheap that is not slippery – cotton or calico perhaps – and get some brightly colored thread. This is so you can see your stitches and monitor how well you are doing.

Prepare to start stitching

First, make sure your machine is set on basic stitch and you have threaded it properly. You should have around four inches of spare thread pulled out so that it can't unthread from the machine. Another thing that will help is if you hold the thread for the first couple of stitches.

Put the fabric underneath the presser foot, making sure the bit you want to stitch is at the front of the machine. Lower the presser foot to hold the fabric in place. This is an easy thing to forget but you'll only do it a few times after your stitches run wild!! Make it your mantra for a while – "lower the presser foot" – and keep on repeating it until you've mastered it.

The upper thread should be on top of the fabric but underneath the presser foot, while the lower thread from the bobbin should be underneath the fabric. Both of the threads should stick out to the back so you are not sewing over them and getting them knotted up.

Before you begin any new line, check that you have lifted the needle up as high as it will go. This will help to stop any of the frustrations of thread that gets stuck or unravels.

Turn on your machine. Lightly put both hands on the fabric on either side of the presser foot. This is to help guide it while sewing. Do not push or pull it and keep your fingers out of the way of the needle – it will hurt! Lower your foot gently onto the pedal and start stitching.

Have lots of practice at this because it's the only way to learn how to guide the fabric and keep your stitching straight and neat.

Once you've got the hang of it, you can start looking at changing your speed. Most machines will have a speed-setting button so you can slow it down or speed it up as you see fit. If your machine is one that does not have a speed setting, you will need to learn how to control speed through the pressure you put on the pedal.

How to use the hand wheel

If you want to sew very slowly or you want to be able to move by just a stitch or two for precision sewing, you can use the hand wheel. Turn it towards you to manually do what the pedal does. You can use the hand wheel to make your first stitch if you like to make sure the thread doesn't unravel or loosen off and to ensure the needle goes where you want it. This is great for controlling the amount the needle moves through the fabric and I use it all the time for finishing off, turning corners, or for precision when doing topstitching.

Cut loose

When you have finished your stitching, raise the presser foot so you can pull the fabric out slightly. Don't forget to raise your needle as well! You do this with the hand wheel if you like; just raise the needle enough to make the thread give a little and you can move the fabric. Then, snip off the threads with small sharp scissors.

Some machines have a handy little blade on the side you can use in one quick move to snip it off but you will need to check the instructions with the book on how to use it.

Securing the stitches

When you start sewing properly, i.e., not during a practice run, you will want to start securing your stitches so they can't come undone. There are two ways to do this:

1. Hold the reverse stitch lever on the machine so you sew backwards a few stitches over the end of the stitches – this is known as "back tacking." Stich forwards again and snip the threads. This is probably the way you will do it most of the time.

2. If you have already sewn off the end of the fabric, simply tie the thread ends together into a double

knot and snip off the ends. You would usually do this when you are sewing darts or in other tricky little spots where you don't want bulky reverse stitching.

Stitching a straight line

Once you have the hang of stitching with the machine, it is time to start learning how to stitch in a straight line. To begin, use a ruler and draw a straight line on the fabric. You can use the needle plate guidelines as well – these will tell you how far the needle is from the edge of the fabric. Take some time to learn how the fabric goes through the machine and how to control it, until you are satisfied that you can sew in a straight line.

Stitching a curved line

When you can sew in a straight line, have a go at sewing in curves. Again, draw a line on your fabric, a nice wavy one, but keep the curves large for now, until you have the hang of it. Put the fabric onto the machine and make sure the presser foot is in line with the first part of the curve.

When you start to sew, gently guide the fabric with your hands and make sure the presser foot remains in line with the upcoming curve. Go slowly; stop as many times as you need to keep up with the curves. This will take practice; so keep going until you are happy your stitching is following the line of your curves.

One thing you might find with curves is that you need to snip the fabric to keep these curves nice and flat. If you are sewing a curved seam, for example, when you turn the item the right way out, there may be areas that are puckered. Snipping the fabric will prevent this from happening.

Turning the corner

Start by drawing a right angle on your fabric. Get the fabric into the machine and start stitching along the line until you get to the corner. At the point of the corner, the needle must be pushed down through your fabric - if it isn't going, use the hand wheel to help it. Raise the presser foot when the needle is in the right place, turn the fabric so the next straight line is in front of you and check that it is parallel to the needle plate guidelines. Put the presser foot back down and continue stitching.

Five Top Tips for Choosing Your First Sewing Project

Before we move on to the final section of the book, which has a few project ideas for you to try out, I want to share my top five tips for choosing the right starter project.

Tip 1 – Keep it simple

Do not head straight for the most complicated pattern you can find; look for something nice and simple. Look for patterns with plenty of straight lines and few pieces. Avoid those with complicated techniques like pleating and gathering until you have some experience. Start slowly and simply, then work your way up to more complicated projects.

Tip 2 – Look at the fabric you need

This is just as important as the actual pattern. Look to make sure the pattern you have chosen can be sewn on easy to use fabric. The very last thing you want to do is choose a pattern that requires a material like silk, which is going to slide everywhere, or a jersey material that stretches and leaves your lines looking unkempt. Choose patterns that can be sewn on medium weight cotton. These are easy to sew, they lie flat, and they don't slide around. They also press well. You can get medium weight cotton in loads of different patterns. Keep in mind; bright patterns can hide dodgy stitching. This tip may or may not be a good thing!

Tip 3 – Avoid Fiddly Patterns

Avoid patterns that require you to put in zips or buttonholes, as these are a bit more complex than straightforward sewing. Choose something with no fasteners or the need to put in sleeves and move on to the more complicated patterns later when you have more experience. You will learn how to do these as part of a natural progression. Keeping it simple means you won't suffer from frustration and will actually be able to finish the projects you are making without too much difficulty.

Tip 4 – Pick a pattern that will fit easily

When you make your own clothes, you can easily tailor them to fit you. We are all different and we all need different things to best flatter our shapes. So, trying to get fitted clothes to fit your curves may not be very easy. Start with simple shapes you can adjust to fit your body. Many patterns are for multiple sizes and need to be cut down to your size. I have shown you in a future chapter how to do this.

Tip 5 – Make it over and over again

Choose a pattern you can see yourself wanting to make over and over again. This helps you to practice the techniques and steps, which will help cement your learning and feel better about the ways you are progressing. This is also useful because when you find something you can make easily, you may even find you can sell it on craft websites such as Etsy and find new ideas for things you can make based on the experience you have gained so far. There are so many interconnected ideas and you will find yourself going from one kind of sewing project to the next, incorporating new ideas as you go.

If you have a particular garment you like but that is worn out, you can also take this apart to make a pattern so you can recreate the garment and get years of use from it. Keep the pattern for future use and if you don't want it in fabric format, buy yourself some paper and make a paper pattern.

Part 3 – Easy Beginner Projects

With the final part of my book, I want to give you some easy projects to try. You can use your sewing machine, you can sew by hand, or you can use a combination of both. Good luck, and above all, have fun!

The Quick Skirt

Materials

- Stretchy fabric in your choice of color and pattern that is wide enough to go around your hips and long enough for however long you want the skirt

- Matching thread

- 1 inch elastic, enough to go around your waist

Drawing your pattern

Get a tape measure and a pad of paper and pencil. Take the following measurements:

- Your waist at its narrowest part

- The widest part, be it your thighs, hips, bottom, stomach, etc.,

- The length you want the skirt to be from the waist

Do not pull the measure tight – the only person you'll be kidding is you – otherwise, your finished skirt will not actually fit the real you. You can always tighten a loose skirt but you can't make a tight skirt looser.

Lay out the fabric you are using. Fold it in half so the printed side, or the right side if it is plain material, is facing inwards and the inside of the skirt is facing outwards. Pin it if necessary to keep it in place.

We'll assume the top edge is going to be the waist, so make sure you cut it straight. Take the measurement you made for the skirt length and add on two inches. Measure from the top of the fabric and go down the material by this amount. Draw a straight line right across the material, using chalk or a disappearing fabric pen. This will be the bottom edge of the skirt so cut along the line and discard the cutoff.

Now, take the measurement you took for your hips and add on three inches. The extra is for seams on the side and to ensure that your skirt is comfortable and you can actually walk in it! Open the fabric out, measure top and bottom by that measurement, and draw a straight line down the fabric between each of the marked points. Make sure it is square and straight and then make your cut.

Fold the fabric in half, making sure it is all lined up and cut it in half. This will give you two pieces of material: the front and back of the skirt.

Fold one piece in half and measure nine inches down from the top edge. Draw a line across the fabric. This is the hip level and will be the widest part of the skirt. If the widest part of your body is different then adjust the levels to match it.

From the top fold, measure a quarter of your waist and then add a ½ inch. For example, if your waist is 28 inches, divide it by 4, which gives you 7, then add on the half inch to get 7 ½ inches. Mark a one-inch line down from the top fold.

Next, comes the curve that will make sure you get a good, flattering fit that doesn't bunch around the waist. Draw a curve that is representative of the curve of your body from hip to waist. Join the point of your hip with the one-inch line you drew and make sure you get a nice curve.

That is your pattern drawn, straight to the fabric with no messing about on paper. Cut along the curve and the line you drew at the waist and make sure you go through both pieces of fabric. Transfer the shape to the other piece of fabric, cut to match, and you have your two skirt pieces.

Sewing your skirt

Place your two pieces of fabric together with the right sides facing each other. Stitch the side from the top down to the bottom and makes sure you get a nice curve at the hips.

Now, press the side seams of the skirt open, turn up the bottom hemline by a ½ inch, and press it. Turn it up again, enclose the edges, and press. Sew around the entire hem using a straight stitch

Take the elastic and put it around your waist, adjusting until it is comfortable. Cut to length. Mark the center and then make another mark a quarter of the way in from the other end. This will give you four even sections. Put the two ends adjacent with each other, making a circle and then stich them with a zigzag stitch.

Fold the skirt so the side seams are together; find the center, both back, and front. Inside the skirt, match the seam in the elastic with one of the side seams and match the center of the elastic with the other side seam. The quarter marks should be matched with the front and back center marks. The elastic will likely be a little smaller than the width of the skirt but that's fine.

Now, stitch the elastic into the skirt waist, keeping it close to the edge. You will need to use a stitch that will stretch, perhaps a triple stretch stitch, a regular zigzag or a 3-step zigzag. Check your manual for this as you sew and stretch the elastic a little to match the fabric if you need.

Turn the elastic over and make a neat edge at the top of the skirt. Stitch it again, going through the elastic so it is held in place.

That's it; your skirt is done. If you are happy with it, make a few more, trying different colors and different lengths.

Make a Pillowcase

These are a fantastic way to use up bits of fabric or old sheets you might have lying around. The finished size should be about 20 inches by 31 inches, which is a standard size. If you have smaller pieces of fabric, you can get clever and use them as borders or embellishments of some kind.

Let's get started

Find a couple of pieces of fabric, doesn't matter what they are. Wash, dry, and then iron them. Fold both pieces in half, which makes it far easier to cut your rectangles.

Cut out a folded rectangle that is 26 inches by 20.5 inches. Because the material is folded in half, you will have two rectangles that are 20.5 by 26 inches with a fold down one side. This will end up as two pieces that are 41 by 26 inches.

Now, cut another folded rectangle of 20.5 inches by 11 inches. Again, you will have two of that size and they will end up as 41 by 11 inches. These are for the border.

Fold the border in half lengthways and iron the fold. You should now have one long strip of material that measures 5.5 inches by 41 inches.

Match the raw edges to the right side of the pillow piece and pin them. Sew the pieces together, using a ½ or ⅜ inch seam allowance.

Iron the seam and then add a top stitch, ⅛ inch over from the edge of the seam to give some extra strength.

Fold the material, right sides facing each other, and then iron the sides and bottom.

Sew down the side and, when you reach the corner, keep the needle in place while lifting the presser foot and turning the fabric. Continue sewing the bottom and then stop, leaving one side open.

Turn the pillowcase inside out, push the corners all the way out and iron the seams. Add any embellishments you want or leave them as they are.

Easy Baby Blanket

You will need:

- One charms pack*

- 1 yard or soft fabric for the bottom of the blanket

- Embroidery floss in a matching color

- Quilting needle

* A charms pack is a pack of fabric precut into 5-inch coordinating squares. Instead of purchasing this pack, you can use any fabric you want that is cut to 5-inch squares.

Instructions

1. Lay your squares out and decide how you want your blanket to look. You can have as many squares as you like.

2. Sew the rows together, starting with square one. Place it facedown on square two, right sides facing, and sew them together on one side with a ¼ inch seam.

3. Continue until you have completed the row and then finish all the other rows the same way.

4. When you are done, press the rows and then sew the rows together in the same way – row one face down on row two, pin and then sew together. Make sure

that you sew the right seams so the blanket is in the order you want it to be in.

5. When all your rows are sewn together, press the whole blanket.

6. Get your baking fabric and cut it so it is the same size as the blanket. Again, right sides together and sew the seam all the way around, but leave a gap of about 4 inches so you can turn it right way out again.

7. Turn it right way out and top stitch all the way around the blanket, making sure to fold the opening under neatly.

8. Thread up your quilting needle with your chosen embroidery thread.

9. At the corners, push the needle down through the top and then tie a square knot up up through the bottom. Do this on all of the corners of all the squares or on every square group of four squares – it's up to you.

That's all there is to making an easy baby blanket. If you feel confident enough, go larger and make yourself one too!

Easy Tote Bag

You can't ever have enough bags and with this pattern, you can make as many as you like, using different fabrics, different colors, patterned or plain. It is very easy to sew and is the perfect beginner's pattern.

You will need

- ½ yard of main fabric

- ⅛ yard of an accent fabric

- ½ yard of inner fabric

- Fusible fleece

- Matching threads

Instructions

Cut the fabric as follows:

- Main fabric – cut out two pieces 13 inches long and 12 inches wide

- Accent fabric – cut out two pieces 12 inches wide and 3 ½ inches long

- Inner fabric – cut out two pieces that are 12 inches wide and 16 inches long

- Main fabric – cut one more piece 3 inches wide and 38 inches long

- Inner fabric – cut one more piece 3 inches wide and 38 inches long

- Fusible fleece – cut two pieces 12 inches wide and 16 inches long and one more piece 3 inches wide and 38 inches long

Begin by placing the accent piece and main piece right sides together and pin, and then sew together.

Iron it flat.

Place the matching fusible fleece pieces to the backs of these pieces and iron it on. Place a cloth over before you iron, otherwise the fleece will stick to the iron, or turn the material over so the fleece is underneath and iron the actual fabric.

To make the strap, iron the fusible fleece onto the wrong side of one strap. Place the straps together so the right sides are facing and sew up either side.

Turn it right side out, press flat, and use a top stitch along the edges.

Put your main pieces right sides together and sew three sides, leaving one of the 12-inch sides open.

Repeat with the inner fabric.

Turn the inner fabric out the right way and push it inside the main fabric.

Stick the strap between the layers, leaving the ends hanging out of the edges.

Sew around the top edge, leaving an opening of a few inches.

Turn it all the right way out; press the edges flat, and top stitch around the top in order to close up the gap.

You officially have one tote bag, ready to use! Have a go at making another with different fabrics and colors.

Placemats

The idea of the placemat is to stitch a template of the elements of the table settings on the fabric. This is a great way to teach your children how to set the table.

This is for a set of 4 placemats.

You will need

- 1 ½ yards of fabric or ¾ yard each of two contrasting fabrics

- Matching thread

- Embroidery floss that is contrasting to the fabric

- A large hand sewing needle

Instructions

Begin by cutting the placemat fabric. You need 8 pieces, each 14 inches by 18 inches. Use all one color or use two colors, one for the back and one for the front.

Separate the pieces into piles for the front and back.

Begin with the front pieces. Place your table utensils on the mat and lightly trace around each one.

Thread the hand needle with the embroidery floss and stitch around the traced utensil. Use a back stich for this and repeat for all four pieces.

Place each front piece with a backing piece, right sides together, and pin them.

Sew around the edge but leave a gap of 4 inches at the bottom*.

Turn the mats right side out and iron flat.

Top stich around the entire edge of the placemat.

Repeat for all of the placemats and trim off any excess thread.

* An alternative method is to turn the placemat right side out, iron it, and then close the opening using a ladder stitch.

JCrew Inspired Tank Top

This is such a simple sewing project and, if you do it right, you will end up with a tank top that looks a bit like a Jcrew top but with a much cheaper price tag.

You will need

- A jersey sheet, any color you like. If you don't have one, you can buy for a few dollars. Or you could just buy some jersey material from the fabric store.

- An old tank top that fits you

- Matching thread

Instructions

Cut the top part of the sheet off but take care not to cut the 2-inch bit that is already folded.

Fold the material in half.

Lay the tank top on the material and trace around it.

Cut around the tracing, but cut about ½ inch too big for the seam allowance.

Pin together the shoulders.

Open up the top bit and cut one side of the neck a little lower than the other.

Fold the material back over.

Sew the shoulders.

Starting under the armhole, sew the seam down to the bottom, and then repeat on the other side

Turn the tank top right side out and finish off the edges.

Take the long strip of material you cut off, set your sewing machine to the highest possible tension, and set it to the longest stitch length.

Stitch the long piece of material. If you have your settings right, you should find it stitches neatly into a ruffle with no need to pull any strings through it to achieve the look.

Starting at the corner, pin the ruffle on the tank top, making a figure eight on one side and then bringing it back up underneath the top ruffle.

Sew down the centerline of the ruffle to attach onto the shirt with a backstitch at either end.

You can actually put the ruffle on in any shape or pattern you want.

Part 4 – Taking Your Sewing a Step Further

In this section, we talk about all the different things you can do with your sewing to take it to another level. Sewing is used for many things and you will find you will use it for mending items or for daily creativity. This section will also help you to learn how to use sewing patterns and, believe it or not, there are patterns specifically made with the beginner in mind. You just need to know what to look for when buying the pattern. We have also come up with some projects you can make involving your kids because when children learn to sew, it means they are pretty much self-sufficient as they grow older. The basic projects we have added to this book under this section will help you to choose the right cottons to be able to mend things when they get damaged and to actually use your imagination to put your sewing skills to good use.

When you are buying a pattern, always look for the expertise level. This is marked on patterns and you can choose those that are geared toward the beginner. There are many to choose from and you really can have a lot of fun with your sewing.

We have also covered some sewing crafts that date back to olden times because if you are going to take on a craft such as sewing, it's nice to have a little background and know how to use the original tools used.

Use of a sewing pattern

In this section, we deal with learning how to use a sewing pattern. When you choose a pattern be very careful and make sure you buy one that covers your level of expertise. You will note sewing patterns are graded according to expertise and will find the symbols on the outside of the pack so you won't easily make a mistake. If in doubt, or if the manufacturer has not marked the skill level on the pack, then ask an assistant who will be able to point you in the direction of beginner patterns.

Choosing your size

It may be prudent to have your size measured so you are completely right when you buy a pattern. If you do have areas where you are a little larger, you can adjust patterns to make up for those discrepancies, but you cannot alter the garment if you have made it too small!

Patterns usually cover a variety of sizes and when you take the pattern out of the pack, you will see that there are various sizes marked on the pattern. If you are one of the smaller sizes, you will have to prepare your pattern and cut it down to the required size. Look at the outlines, as these clearly mark to which size of garment that particular line refers. When you are cutting out your pattern be careful to respect all markings and make sure you do not cut over the lines.

Buying your fabric

The type of fabric you use should be that suggested by the pattern makers. There will be a chart on the back of the pattern that shows you how much fabric you need for which particular size. I always buy a little more than I need to take account of mending at a later date but also because everyone can make mistakes when cutting out. As fabric is not terribly expensive, it doesn't hurt to be prudent. Fabrics to avoid if you are new to sewing are stretch fabrics and expensive silks, as these may get caught up in your sewing machine if you are inexperienced. Cottons and viscose fabrics are very easy to work with.

Buying your cotton

If they do not have the exact color that you are looking for, you need to buy a shade darker. This may sound strange, but when cotton is all reeled up, it actually looks darker than when in single strands. Thus, buying a shade darker will ensure your cotton is the right color for your fabric.

Pinning out your pattern

You will need to respect the way the fabric is woven. This is called the nap. There is a good reason for this. If you don't respect the nap, you may find that the garment will stretch over time. On the pattern, arrows denote the nap and these arrows must be placed on the fabric so they follow the weave of the fabric.

Lay out your fabric on a flat surface. If there are parts of the pattern where you need to cut two identical pieces but which form different sides of the pattern, then folding the fabric in half will help you to achieve this.

Pin your pattern with sewing pins and at this stage, don't cut anything out until all the pieces of the pattern are laid out and you are sure about seam allowance. Some patterns allow for this and others do not, so read your pattern. This is very important. If you need to make a seam allowance outside of the given pattern, then you need to leave enough space. Make your cut a ¼ inch to a ½ inch wider than the pattern if no seam allowance is made. I tend to make this a wider seam allowance if the fabric is likely to fray. That way, I can hem each side of the seam to ensure this does not happen.

The pins should be sufficient to keep the fabric neatly in place. It's better to use more than to skimp as this will hold the fabric still while you are cutting.

Markings that you need to be aware of

There may be markings that need to be transferred onto the fabric and there is a special stitch used for this. For example, a dart is where the fabric is folded to create a shape. On all patterns you will see the symbol ● and this is where you need to make a stitch. To make this stitch, thread up a needle with double thread and then sew down into the dot and up again, then repeat this so you have a loop. This loop should be reasonably loose because in order to ensure the mark is on both pieces of fabric, you will separate the fabric and cut the loop in between the pieces of fabric. Thus, the stitch that is left shows you where this symbol is, so that you can use these marks to do whatever it is the pattern intends.

Cutting out your fabric

When you are cutting out, make sure you have allowed for a seam allowance if the pattern has not marked one. Cut with good quality sewing shears and use a hard surface, so the fabric does not get wrinkled during the process.

Sewing order

If you have darts on the garment, these need to be done before you do the seams. To make a dart, you will have the marks where you made the stitches and will be able to fold the dart and iron it before stitching it with your sewing machine. These start at the edge of the garment and work inward to a point. Be careful to draw a line so your dart is perfectly straight and fasten off your thread when you have finished sewing. You can also take out the tacking thread you used to mark the dart when you cut out the garment.

Using the markings on your sewing machine bed

The markings that fall under the foot of the machine are there for a purpose. They tell you the distance between the seam you are sewing and the edge of the material. When you are sewing two pieces together, the right side of the fabric should be inward and you should respect the same distance from the foot of the machine at all times so your lines are straight. If you are a real beginner and you want to be sure that your lines are really good, you can mark these onto the fabric with tailor chalk but you shouldn't need to if you are using the guide below the foot.

Tips for different processes during the sewing project

It is much easier to work if you iron each process after its completion. For example, if a dart needs to go downward, iron it down before you sew the seam. When you have sewn a seam, iron the seam on the wrong side so you have a neat edge for hems. I find that ironing each section as I do it keeps my work a lot neater and means I can see clearly where I need to stitch for the next process.

Stiffening

This is something you may be asked to use and the best type to buy is the iron-on type. This is used in collars, for example, and is ironed onto the fabric on the wrong side. What this does is give a stiffness to certain areas of your garment, such as collars, cuffs, button trims, etc., and it's a good practice to make sure you do this as you work so you are ready for the next stage of sewing.

French seams

These are seams with no raw edges. Although you need a little more seam allowance, these are worth trying out with a scrap of fabric because when you are using fabrics that fray, this will stop that from happening and will also give a rather neat seam with no raw edges.

Take two pieces of fabric and place them with the back of the fabric facing the back of the fabric, or with the good side showing on the outside. Sew a seam which joins the two pieces together and this seam should respect the ¼ inch standard. Then, turn the fabric the other way out so the raw seam faces inward. Trim off any excess and create another seam on the other side that obscures the original seam. What you end up with is a very neat seam on the outside and a folded seam in the inside.

This kind of seam is very useful for skirts, blouses, pants, and all kinds of garments where you don't want seams to fray.

Hemming with a machine

There are machines that will do blind hemming and if you are fortunate enough to have one of these, I would suggest you try with a scrap of fabric before you do this to your finished garment, as it takes a little while to get used to where the needle has to be on the fabric. If you are sewing hems on jeans, where topstitching is used elsewhere on the garment, you can actually get away with ordinary stitching for the hem and simply whizz these through the machine using the same color thread as the top stitching. Your jeans will look a lot more professional if they are dealt with in this way since blind hemming is not usually used for jeans.

Making Basic drapes

The homemaker will want to make curtains at some time. Moving house and making things yourself can be very satisfying. The instructions given here will help you to make the perfect drapes and they really are not difficult to make at all, even if you use a lining to stop the fabric from becoming discolored during hot months or to keep the house warm during the winter.

Measuring up for curtains

You need to measure the width of the window and bear in mind, curtains are usually larger than the window's size because of the gathering you use and because the curtain rail comes out beyond the actual size of the window. I always use one and a half times the width measured so that I have plenty of gathering fabric. If you want a lot of gathering, you can double the width to ensure you have loads of fabric.

Then you need to measure the drop. This will be from the rail to the floor. Add to that drop enough fabric for a hem at the top and at the bottom of the fabric because this will be needed to ensure your curtains look nice. You will need six inches for the bottom hem and a seam allowance of about two inches for the top. For the sides of the curtain you need to add an inch each side of the curtain to ensure that you have adequate fabric.

Choosing headings

The headings you use do matter because these dictate whether you need to buy 1.5, 2.00 or 2.5 times the width of the window. These come in a tape format and it's wise to ask the assistant in the shop how much extra fabric you need to buy in order to use the tape you have chosen.

Cutting out curtains

When you are cutting out items as large as curtains, you do need a flat surface. If you don't have a flat surface you are likely to cause creases in your fabric, which mess up your cutting. Laying them on the floor will be fine if the floor is clean. The flatter the fabric, the better. You need to cut out sufficient curtains for the room in question. For now, we are simply making unlined curtains because you can learn about linings later on.

If a fabric lays a certain way, mark the top so you don't mess this up. Since your seam at the top is going to be smaller than the hem, this is important. Cut out the curtains and take them to the ironing board. In order to make your hems down the side of the curtains as neat as possible, iron the hems into place before they are sewn. Many people use invisible stitch for the sides of the curtains, as this is the best stitch to hide. Fold the hem once to get rid of raw edges and then fold it again, but make sure the hem on the sides of the curtains is relatively narrow. I tend to use a ¼ inch or even less for the side hems on curtains. These are not structural and are not quite as important as the hems.

To invisible stitch the hems

This is a lot easier to do if you have already pressed the hems into place. Thread your needle and start your work with a double stitch so your thread is held in place. Now, working on the back of the curtains, place the hem over your knee and take the needle down into the outer fabric, picking up a single thread of fabric before bringing the needle up through the hem. Move along the hem a little and do the same thing. Try to keep your stitches neat. You should not actually see the stitching on the right side of the fabric. Work all of your upright edge hems on your curtains.

Top hem and heading

There is a very good reason for doing the top hem before the lower hem. This is because when you hang the curtains, you may need to adjust your lower hem to suit the location. The top hem, however, is vital to hanging the curtains. Fold over the top hem. This should be about four inches, rather than the six at the bottom. Press it.

Now, take your header tape. You will need to fold it at the ends so there are no raw edges. Pin it into place with about a ¼ inch of fabric above it. This ensures the tape is not seen on the right side of the curtains. Pin it at both the top and bottom, since you need to machine stitch across the top and bottom of the tape to keep it neatly in place. Baste it into place with contrasting thread so you can pull out the basting once the machine stitching is done.

Machine stitch the tape in place, making sure that both ends of the tape are folded in and neat. Finish off your machine stitching either by using the reverse stitch to secure your last stitch or by pulling the thread through and tying it off.

Your curtains are almost done when you reach this stage. The only thing you have left is the bottom hem. Before you sew this, hang the curtains, because this gives you an accurate marking of where you want your bottom hem to fall.

Marking your hem

To mark the hem, use your sewing pins and pin the hem up at one end so it is just above floor level and does not drag onto the floor. If your curtains are simply to be over the window and do not go to floor level, mark the hem where you require it to be. This is usually just below the sill so when the curtains are closed, you do not see the window structure. When you have pinned the correct length, you can take the curtain to the ironing board and iron the hem.

A hem is made up of two folds; one at the correct length and the other to tuck in the raw edges of the fabric. Make sure you iron this neatly and check your measurements, as these are vital to the quality of the finish.

Sewing your hem

This is worked in invisible stitch because you don't really want to see the stitching on the right side of the curtains. Thus, use invisible stitch as described above to secure the hem on the bottom of the curtain.

Adding a lining to new curtains

If you want to make curtains that have linings, the process is a little different. Your lining fabric will be cut a little narrower than your curtain fabric and instead of sewing hems up the side of the curtains, you will simply sew the lining to the curtain fabric, then turn it the right way out, and press it. The fact that your lining is narrower than your curtain will mean you will have a neat line of the original curtain fabric showing on each side next to the lining on the wrong side of the curtain. Before I sew linings into a curtain, I tend to pin them and always make sure the seam is measured so there are no bulky areas. If you are doing this for the first time, pin your lining to the front side of the curtain fabric and mark your line so that your sewing is very accurate. When both side seams have been sewn, take the curtain to the ironing board and press so the exposed fabric at each side of the lining is exactly the same width on each side.

The rest of the procedure is much the same for the header but when you come to do the hem of the curtain, there is a difference. Fold your normal hem at six inches. Then, bring your lining over the top and cut it so you can machine stitch a hem for the lining which drops above the actual hem of the curtains so you don't see it on the outside. Then invisible stitch your hem and sew in any areas that may need it to give your curtains a really nice finish.

I cannot over emphasize how important ironing is when you are making large items such as curtains. You make all of your seams much straighter and your hems perfect by having ironed them into place before stitching.

Darning a Sock

This is a project you can enjoy because you may just have a favorite pair of socks you don't want to part with, but which have a hole. The reason I chose this project is because it helps you to understand how fabrics are constructed. In fact, what you are going to do is construct fabric where there is none by filling the hole in the sock so it can continue to be used. There is one extra tool you will need for this and that's a sock mushroom. This is a mushroom-shaped tool used for darning. When placed inside the sock with the hole positioned on top of the mushroom you can clearly see the damage.

You will need some wool or some thread which is the same color as the sock and a needle with an eye large enough to take that thread. If you were using wool, for example, you would use a darning needle because the eye is larger and able to take the thread easily. This is the same kind of needle that you would use to sew up knitted garments.

With the needle threaded, make a whole row or running stitches around the edge of the hole. This is to solidify the edge so that the hole does not become larger. Then taking your needle across the hole, create a thread that is drawn over the hole, but be careful not to pull this tight, and the garment should remain flat. You make a series of stitches like this that spread across the hole and form a grid of lines. These are the upward facing lines in this diagram. Then take your needle and weave those lines in the other direction, over a thread and then under a thread, over a thread and under a thread. What you are creatively doing is making fabric where there is no fabric by weaving through the lines that you originally created.

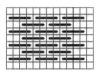

Sewing on a Button

You may think this is relatively straightforward, but you would be surprised how many people get this wrong. You do need to have button thread if you want your buttons to stay in place. If the button has holes that show on the outside, choosing a color of thread that suits the rest of the buttons is ideal. Otherwise the garment will look untidy.

Thread your needle and make sure the needle is capable of going through the holes in the button. As some buttons only have a small hole, you will need to adjust to the size that works with the size of the buttonholes. Double stitch the back of the garment to start and bring the needle up in the right position for the button. Put the needle through the buttonhole and then back down again through the other hole. Some buttons have four holes and you can either sew these with a cross shape or you can use a pair of the holes and then the other pair of the holes so there is no cross in the center. Look at the garment as your guide because you need to follow the same pattern as used already.

Your needle is taken through the fabric and brought up through the holes and down through the other hole in your chosen sequence about half a dozen times. Then, instead of pushing the needle through the button the next time, bring the needle up between the button and the garment rather than taking it all the way through.

Now, twist the thread around your stitches about six times. This is done with your hand, simply winding the thread around the stitches between the button and the fabric. Take the needle and place it through all of these stitches and pull the thread through. Put the needle through the stitches from the other side in the same manner.

Now, push the needle through to the back of the work and double stitch to finish. All of this helps to secure the button and since buttons get a lot of wear and tear, this ensures it will stay in place. Often buttons are sewn onto a garment with a machine and are prone to fall off if the work is not tied off. On many factory-produced items this is the case.

Patching a worn garment

When your child's jeans have a hole in the knee and these are only used for play, you can lengthen their life by learning to use colorful patches on the patch. You have a choice of whether to use a contrasting patch as a decorative element or whether to save old jeans so you have fabric on hand for such a scenario. Cut out the size of the patch you require, bearing in mind you will need a hem all the way around this patch so raw edges are not visible.

It is quite hard to machine stitch a patch onto the leg of children's jeans because you don't have the facility to get inside the leg to hold everything in place. Take your patch and iron a hem all the way around it so it is nice and flat. Then, pin the patch in place so you are happy with its placement. If you use a blanket stitch as described in this book, you can make a really nice decorative element of the patch by choosing a contrasting thread. If you want more discreet patches, then you can still use blanket stitch, though use a thread that hides in with the color of the garment.

Taking clothing in a size

The best way to take clothing in a size is to actually turn the garment inside out. This gives you access to where all the seams are. Have the person the garment belongs to try it on and use your dressmaking pins to pin the seams in where you need to take off excess fabric. With shirts, you need to be aware the sides of the shirt will join with the sleeves, so you may need to take a little off the width from the sleeve as well to make the garment look neat on the outside. If you are taking off a lot of the size, then you will need to trim the seams once they are done so there is not bulk fabric inside the garment, making it uncomfortable to wear.

After you have pinned the alterations, baste them and get the wearer to try the item on the right way out. This shows you where any other additional alterations need to be made. Use your dressmaking pins to note these areas and when the garment is all basted and correct, use your sewing machine to take the seams in with straight stitch. With some garments, it's easier to unpick the original seams because when ironed, you can actually get a much neater finish.

Taking up Hems

This is something you will do on a regular basis. It's normal you buy things and then find that they need adjustment to your size. Thus, learning how to take up hems is very useful. For jeans, for example, you need to pin the hem at the required length and cut off the excess fabric. There is a reason for this, because jeans fabric is very thick and will look bulky otherwise. When you are adjusting the length of hems on jeans and have cut off the excess fabric, you need to mark the correct length and then iron the hems, folding over a tiny bit on the inside, so you don't have raw edges. Think of hems as being folded over and then folded over again. Jeans hems are not wide. They should be about quarter of an inch or at least in line with other top stitching on the same garment. The cotton should be the same color.

When you are happy with the lengths, baste them and get your machine threaded with the right color thread. Everyone will see the top stitch. You should always start at the inside of the leg, where the threads can be hidden and work your way around the hem neatly, making sure the fabric is always kept straight in the machine as you work. Crooked stitching really doesn't look good.

At the end of the hemming, do a reverse stitch to secure the thread and then tie off any loose thread. Press the hem.

Hems on dresses

These may be more complex. It really depends upon the style of dress and the type of fabric. Always use the way the manufacturers chose when you are taking up a hem on a dress. For example, if invisible stitch was used in the original construction, it was for a purpose and you need to adhere to the same invisible stitches when you take up the hem. If, however, top stitch was used, then this should be respected. In addition, you will need to make sure you have the same color of cotton available for the hemming.

Measure from the waist of the garment down to where you have placed a pin to indicate the required length. Fold the fabric up and pin it in place. You need to take all of your measurements from the waist, straight down to the hem, and pin the whole hem before you even consider cutting the fabric. Once pinned, you will see how much fabric you have and will be able to decide how much of it to cut off, bearing in mind your hem needs to be folded twice and should be the same height as the original hem so the dress does not look altered.

Iron your hem and cut off the excess, folding the hem as you do so and making sure it is all the same height. At this stage, you can use dressing-maker pins but do not baste the hem until you have had the wearer try it on to see how it hangs. Then, baste the hem and you are ready to sew.

If topstitch was used on the original, then this is done with the machine, but be careful to guide the hem through the machine so as not to cause any puckering in the fabric. Taking it slow will ensure your work is neat and tidy. It's worth taking this extra time. If the hem is hand-stitched, this is done with invisible stitch on the inside of the garment.

Mending torn seams

Quite often, people are disappointed about the quality of items they buy. The seams are not that well sewn and often stitching can come out. I suppose this is part and parcel of cheaply done mass production. If you do have a garment where the seam has come undone, you need to fix it as soon as possible. You will need to have a thread the same color used on the original garment and will first need to iron the seam so you can see clearly where the stitches need to start and finish.

Once this is established, use your sewing machine to work over the place where the stitches have started to fail. It's not enough to simply sew where they have failed because they will continue to fail unless you do this. Begin stitching and take your stitching down below where the problem started so both ends of the mend are secure and unlikely to cause future problems.

Learning to use decoratively a blanket stich

A Blanket stitch is a very good stitch to learn because it gives you a lot of scope with your sewing work. Taking a simple sweater and turning it into a designer sweater is as simple as choosing the right color by using blanket stitch to give the garment the extra trimming it lacked.

I want to explain blanket stitch for several reasons. It's one of the nicest stitches you can use because it finishes off edges and gives great definition to different areas of clothing, blankets, kitchen linen, etc., and is a traditional stitch young girls used to learn in order to have the ability to run their household. Of course, this was only one small part of what they learned, but it's a part that has been useful to people who enjoy sewing. It's not only decorative;

it's also very practical for putting two pieces of fabric together.

In this section, I am not only going to show you how to use blanket stitch, I am going to give you several projects ideas good for showing off the blanket stitch, so you can share your craft with your friends and family.

Materials needed:

- An old sweater

- Contrasting wool

- A darning needle

- Scissors

Thread your needle with your chosen color. Blanket stitch is worked in a very neat way, being sure all of your stitches are the same length and the same distance apart. For this project, we are going to work on the hem of a sweater. This makes a great surface to see the true nature of a blanket stitch. If you don't like it, you will be able to pull it out and you won't harm the sweater, so you can practice this on an old sweater without worrying about spoiling it.

Tie a knot in the end of your thread so it won't come through. It's actually a better practice to learn to do a double stitch on the wrong side of the work to start your work off correctly, so if you want to try this, the explanation is easy. Turn to the inside of your work. Take your needle in and out so the wool won't show on the outside of the garment and then do the same again, pulling it tightly, so you have anchored your thread.

Blanket stitch

With a blanket stitch what you are doing is pulling your needle up through the work to the right side of the garment about quarter of an inch from the actual edge of the neckline. Then, place the needle downward into the neckline in line with the place where your needle came upward. This creates a loop. Pull your needle through this loop. Then, take the needle a little further along in line with the other stitches and put it down through the fabric and bring it through the loop. Each stitch is exactly the same and takes the same order. It should also respect distance, so your stitches are really neat and tidy.

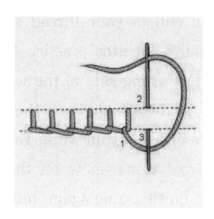

In the image above, you will see that the edge of the neck is actually the edge shown as the lower edge. This is a wonderful stitch for beginners to learn because the finish you create looks so professional. Work your way all around the collar of your garment and you will see it really does look nice. As I said, this is really a practice run, but I wanted to show you it because there are so many applications for which you can use this stitch. The edge of a knitted blanket, for example, for a baby blanket will always look better if you can sew around it using a blanket stitch in a contrasting color.

Christmas decorations

These are easy to make using blanket stitch and I would suggest you have wool in either green, gold, or white and you buy some pieces of felt and a length of ribbon. You will also need a star shape and if you are not much good at drawing, go to Google images and look for printable star shapes to print these off and use one as your pattern. Red felt is the best to use because it is a great contrast to the Christmas tree, although you could also use green felt and red wool as a contrast. I did some of these with gold thread that actually twinkled against the lights of the tree and they were very attractive indeed. The gold thread can be bought in the embroidery department of your local store or online.

Cut out two stars, as what the blanket stitch is going to do is to sew these together. This is something children can participate in because the needle used is relatively large and not too difficult for tiny hands, though do make sure the child is supervised and not of the age where he or she will tend to put things in his or her mouth.

Place both shapes together and begin your blanket-stitching by doing a double stitch on the inside of one of the pieces of felt. That way, you don't get to see the end when you put the two pieces of felt together. Your stitches should be very neat and always use a contrasting color because that's what gives the work its crisp appearance. When you have done blanket stitch all around the star, you should have reached a tip of the star. Sew pieces of ribbon in place before double stitching your thread off to finish the star.

Christmas Stockings

Christmas stockings are always going to be popular with kids and why not get them to help make their own? For these, you need sufficient felt to make the sides of the stocking but you can also add fabric that contrasts it at the top of the stocking. This can be stitched into place using simple stitching, like a running stitch, or you can merely use a glue to put it onto the top of the stocking.

When you are happy with your fabrics and the stockings are all cut out and ready to sew, use your blanket stitch, by starting at the front of the stocking so when you have finished the blanket stitch all the way around the stocking, you arrive at the back of the ankle of the stocking where you can sew in a ribbon or a colorful string that can be used to hang the stocking.

Making Home-made tea towels and cloths

Since you may have fabrics around the house that are no good any more for their given purpose, these can be repurposed. For example, worn sheets can be turned into useful cloths or tea towels. Cut them out and then take them to the ironing board. I always hem things with the iron before I actually sew them because this means the hems are so much neater. This is also a project you can do with kids because it really doesn't matter if they make a mess of it. The materials have not cost you a lot of money.

The hems you use should be double folded so there are no raw edges showing, but all you need to do is to actually iron these into place. The blanket stitch will do the rest and that's good news for you, as you will be hemming and decorating the pieces at the same time.

Use blanket stitch all around the cloth and make sure you enfold the hem that you have ironed into the stitch so the hem is held firmly in place. These make great additions to gift baskets for grandma or for people who are just moving into a new home. Although they are made from scraps of fabric, dusters, tea towels, and cloths are things that every household needs and will always be welcome as a gift.

10 Advanced Sewing Techniques Every Sewer Should Know

All sewers, experienced or new, dream of being able to produce the perfect garment: a beautiful dress for a party, tailored trousers, the perfect skirt and jacket for a big interview. All of these garments have one thing common – they all require the use of advanced techniques. It doesn't matter what level of machinist you are, whether you have one day or a year of experience under your belt, the following are 10 of the top advanced techniques all sewers should learn.

1. Trim and Piping

These are like the garnish on a cordon bleu meal; they are not needed but they do add something quite special to the finished product. Seams or edges that are smoothly piped can give a good deal of emphasis to the design and lines of a pattern, or they can be used to add a contrasting color, like white trim on a black jacket.

You can buy piping from your craft store or you can use a piping or zipper foot to produce your own. Trims are the ideal way of accenting one color from a boucle or printed fabric, and you can sew these on using your machine or by hand. Learn these techniques by practicing on cheap fabrics to start with and then try adding a trim to the neck of a jacket or piping to a skirt waistband.

2. Welt Pockets

Many of the best jackets and coats have got welt pockets. You also see them on trousers on pencil skirts and even on some purses. Once you get the hang of this technique you will want to put them on everything. There are loads of variations, including the single welt, the double welt, the welt with a flap, and even the welt with a zipper. Once you have learned the basic technique, it is dead easy to adapt and you can modify the basic welt pocket to fit any pattern or any fabric:

Basic Single Welt Pocket

- Cut your welt from your chosen material. It should be the length of the pocket, plus an additional inch, and twice the width of the pocket size you want, plus an additional inch.

- You will also need two pieces of pocket material, matching and contrasting threads, and either tailor's chalk or a water erasable marker.

- Fold the welt in half lengthways with the right side facing each other. Sew up the short ends leaving a seam allowance of a ¼ inch.

- Clip the corners at the top so you reduce the bulk.

- Turn the welt right side out and press it.

- Use a contrasting thread and baste the welt together, a ½ inch from the raw edge.

- Then, baste a ¼ inch seam at the top edge of the first pocket piece.

- Use the chalk or marking pen to mark out where the pocket opening will be on the right side of the garment. It should be equal to the finished welt size. Mark the center of the placement with a horizontal line.

- Line the raw edges of the welt with the centerline on the right side of the garment. Right side down, line the basted edge of the pocket piece on the top half of the line you marked for the center. Pin the welt and the pocket piece to hold their places.

- Stitch the welt along the contrasting stitch line to hold it in place and then stitch the pocket piece along the contrasting stitch to hold that in place too; you can now remove the basting stitches.

- Flip the garment to the wrong side and cut through the middle line, making sure to stop half an inch from each end. Clip the ends so they are a Y shape; later on you will sew the triangles down.

- Push the pocket through and adjust it so it lays flat. Press it and then turn up the welt and press that.

- Right side down, sew the second pocket piece along the raw edge of the welt, attaching the two together.

- Fold back the fabric and sew those triangles to the pocket. You may need to use the zipper foot if your fabric is bulky.

- Sew the pocket together and then finish off your edges – the quickest option is to pink them, as this doesn't add extra bulk.

- Right side of the garment, hand stitch the shortest edges of the welt to the actual garment.

That completes a basic single welt pocket.

3. Underlining

There are a number of reasons why you might want to add an underlining to your garment, depending on the type of material you used. If you are using a lightweight silk fabric, an underlining can add some strength to the garment and help to reduce the number of wrinkles. If you add an underlining to a wool dress, it can cut out the need to use facings. Adding an underlining to a garment gives structure and allows the outermost fabric to shine and be the real star of the show. It is a great technique for the intermediate sewer to try, using a wide range of different hand-stitches inside the garment.

4. Complex Construction

There are patterns that can be a real maze of markings and it isn't always easy to transfer that to your fabric. Learning how to do that will be one of the biggest skills for you to master. With complex designs, paying close attention and using precision on even the smallest of details will result in fantastic designs and some very intriguing shapes translated to fabric. Take a look at some of the more beautiful vintage patterns and you will see that they have darts or complex pleating you just don't see on modern patterns. One of the best ways to get into complex construction could be to add a structured sleeve to a simple dress or jacket.

5. Traditional Tailoring

We all want to come up with one garment that is going to last for years, especially the time-honored jacket. Using a hair padding interface, pad stitching, lots of steam, and just a little patience you can create a jacket you can wear with a pair of jeans or with your favorite skirt or dress and that will stay up to date and in style for many years. Producing a traditionally tailored garment is a real investment of time and is a good way to build up your repertoire of essential sewing skills.

6. Using Bias Tape

Bias tape, otherwise known as bias binding, is a long fabric strip that has been cut on the bias, or diagonally, to maximize the stretch of the garment. It is used on armholes and necklines and ensures the tape stretches around the seams.

You can buy bias tape or you can make your own. These steps involve the use of store bought bias tape being inserted into armholes. You would use the same steps for necklines and hems on shirts and dresses.

- Take your bias tape and press the centerfold flat. Make sure you press several feet of the tape but do not take it off the cardboard it is packaged on. Later on, you can cut it to length once it has been sewed into the armhole.

- Press one edge of the bias top flat.

- Beginning at the seam of the armhole, place the bias tape with one inch extending beyond the seam. You should have the raw edges of the tape and the material positioned and aligned with the right sides facing.

- Pin the tape around the armhole, inserting a pin every two inches or so. Stretch the tape a little as you pin it so it curves easily around the armhole.

- Once you have pinned it all the way around, trim the tape so there's one inch extending out from the seam. You should have two tails of the tape that are about the same length.

- Align the tails with the bias tape seam entered over the armpit seam on the armhole. Put a pin through both layers of the tape but NOT through the garment material. Place the pin perpendicular where the tails meet and are sitting flat on the fabric.

- Start to sew the tape to the garment, about one inch ahead of the seams on the tape and armpit. Use a backstitch and a ⅜ inch seam allowance, enabling the stitch to go down the crease you ironed out earlier. Make sure you remove the pins as you sew.

- Continue around the whole armhole, and stop around one inch from the seam and the backstitch. Leave the perpendicular pin holding the tape tails together.

- Take the garment out from under the presser foot and cut the threads. Pull the tape tails away from the material and then sew a vertical stitch down the shot bias tape where the pin was. Backstitch up the tape once, making sure you are not touching the material of the garment.

- Trim the tails to a ¼ inch and lay the tape flat against the pin and material.

- Sew the unstitched part of the tape to the fabric using the same seam allowance, making sure the seams on the tape and armpit align.

- Press the tape away from the material, ensuring your seam allowance is pressed away from the inside of the garment.

- Stitch ⅛ inch from the seam on the right side of the bias tape. We call this under stitching. This gives you the nice armhole that stays flat and hides the bias tape. You should get into the habit of under stitching every time you use bias tape, otherwise the tape could end up showing.

- Turn the garment inside out and press the tape firmly to the inside and pin it every two inches.

- Secure the tape by sewing it with a ⅛ inch seam allowance from the inside edge, starting at the armpit seam.

- Turn the garment right side out again and press the armholes.

That completes an armhole using bias tape; now give it a go on necklines as well.

7. Topstitching

Topstitching sounds simple and, in all fairness, it is. Topstitching gives your garments a finished look; a look that we take for granted and seriously underestimate. Try making a top without topstitching, take a long hard look at it and then add the topstitch. You will see what I mean. If you have an edge-stitching foot, use it to create a straight topstitch line. If you can go for heavy weight topstitching threads as this, will give you a much bigger, more visual impact. Do make sure your machine tension is absolutely spot on, as this stitch is going to be the focal point of your garment.

Top Stitching Tips

Because the thread in a top stitch is completely visible, it is vital that everything about it is spot on.

Thread Weight

While all-purpose threads are great for just about any project, you should give the specialty threads a go as well. Topstitch thread tends to be heavier and thicker than other threads and is often called "heavy duty" thread. You will see the visual difference between normal and heavy-duty stitch straight away. However, thread weight really comes down to your personal preference. You may want lighter topstitches that blend in, in which case, you can use a universal thread. On the other hand, if you want your top stitches to be the first thing people see, use the proper topstitch thread. Experimentation is the key here and, until you have a go with both types, you won't know what you prefer. Bear in mind, certain top stitches will suit certain garments better.

One note: if you are using a proper topstitch thread, you do not need to fill up the bobbin with the same thread. Just use a universal thread in the same color.

Needles

If you opt for the proper topstitch thread, you will need to use a topstitch needle. These have a much larger eye, which makes it easier for getting the thread through. Topstitch needles also tend to be a little larger all over and have a much sharper point to make it easier to go through six layers – four materials and two interfacing.

Foot

You can use the default foot on your sewing machine for topstitching without any trouble. However, there is a foot called a blind hem foot that works really well for topstitching. Take a look at one and you will see a small piece of metal extending out from under the base of the foot. That is what lines up with the seam edge and, when you have moved the needle to the right by one step, it will sew a dead-straight topstitch line. It will have a smaller seam allowance than a universal foot but it is much faster.

So, you can use all-purpose universal thread and a universal sewing machine foot, or you can use proper topstitch thread and blind hem foot for your topstitching. How you do it is down to how your preferences. If you are topstitching heavy materials, you might find the proper thread and the blind hem foot works best, while for a more delicate kid of fabric, the universal method might give better results. Again, experiment and find out which is best.

8. Zippers

One of the most important of all the skills you need to learn is how to apply a zipper, no matter what type it is. Inserting a zipper properly will give your finished work a more professional look. Although, if you get the zipper wrong, your work will look homemade and poorly made at that. The key to this is knowing all of the steps involved before you start and make sure you do the right preparation before you begin stitching. The right marking, placement, and basting will all help ensure your zippers are centered correctly, that your stitching is done nice and straight and evenly, and that everything starts and ends where it should. Many commercial patterns are very oversimplified in their instructions and often miss out the small details that are vital to the project.

For some people, sewing in zippers is a huge challenge. Each application will have its own techniques and rules but there are some standardized tips that can help you make sure every zip is sewn in properly and looks professionally done.

Preparing to sew

The first step is obviously to buy a zipper but it is vital that you make sure it is the right zipper and the color and size for the project. If you can't find a zipper right length, go for one that is a little longer than the seam opening it is going into. This gives you a bit of room for positioning it and will stop you from hitting the end stop on the zipper with the needle, which would cause it to break.

Do wash the zipper before you sew it in to stop it from shrinking, especially if the zipper is made from natural materials.

Press the zipper on the fabric side; making sure it is as flat as you can get it and using a gentle heat so the teeth wont melt if the zipper is plastic.

Take some lightweight fusible interfacing and cut it into strips as long as the seam and one-inch-wide if you are using lightweight material not strong enough to stand up to a zipper. The interface strengthens the material to allow it to stand up to the repetitive pressure of an opening and closing zipper.

Put the interface into the seam area of your garment. You should have received instructions with your fusible interface, so follow those. All you are doing is putting the strips of interface on the wrong side of the garment fabric, beside the seam. Then, you need to iron over both the interfacing and fabric, thus sealing the interfacing onto the material.

Sewing the Zipper in

First, you must close the opening for the zipper by machine basting it. Sew along the edge where the zipper is going to be placed and remember to keep your seam allowances in line with the rest of the garment. While this might seem to be a waste of time, keep in mind that a baste stitch is temporary and is only being used to keep the seam in place; it will be removed once the zipper has been attached.

Press open the seam, pressing the seam allowance against the wrong side of the garment. Try to get these as flat and open as you possibly can because the folds on each side of the basting stitch have to be as crisp as you can get them.

Now, pin the zipper in place. Close the zipper and put it into position, with the pull sitting at the top just above the top line of your garment. It doesn't matter if there is an excess of zip below the seam end; though you will need about an inch of excess hanging down, the rest can be trimmed off. Cut off any excess before the zipper is pinned on and whip stitch the end to make the stop.

Next, machine baste the zipper in. Again, this stitch will be removed later on; you are only using it to hold the zipper in place. These stitches are necessary because they will make sure that the zipper teeth are centered on the seam as you sew it on.

Turn the garment over so the right side is upwards and check to make sure you can only see the top of the zipper. The rest of the zipper should be hidden.

Use the zipper foot on your sewing machine to topstitch the seam through all four layers. Start sewing from the bottom to the top on each side to stop it from rippling. Keep the stitches as near to the center of the seam as you possibly can. Finish off with a line of stitches running across the bottom of the seam to give a stop point the zipper cannot go past.

Lastly, remove the basting stitches using a seam ripper. Start with the ones that held the zipper in place and then go on to the ones going down the center of the seam. Be careful you don't snag any of the material thread or any of the topstitches. While the seam ripper is a handy tool, it can cut threads you don't want cut, so watch what you are doing.

Test the zipper and make sure that it easily slides up and down and is properly centered in the seam.

9. Sewing with Elastic

Elasticated waists were all the rage at one point and they are fast making a comeback. It is an important skill to learn because at some point you will want to put an elasticated waist on a pair of comfortable pajamas or a skirt. Here's how to sew in an elastic waistband:

- Following your pattern insertions, cut the elastic to fit around the body part it is going around. For an elasticated waist, use one-inch elastic and cut it to fit your natural waist. Use the right type and size of elastic recommended by the pattern designer.

- Sew the ends of the elastic together by overlapping the ends and pinning them in place. Overlap by one inch to be sure.

- Use a straight stitch to sew the ends together, then backstitch each of the stitches. Pull in the elastic to make sure it is secured.

- Start where the ends overlapped and fold the elastic in half. This is so you can find the spot exactly opposite the overlap. Mark the spot. Now, put the overlap and the opposite spot together. Find the halfway point between them, marking the spots so you have four sections, each of equal size. Mark the spots with pins, inserted vertically into the elastic.

- Now, repeat the above step with the waistband on your garment, starting from the center of the back as your starting point.

- Put the elastic onto the wrong side of your material, making sure the top of the elastic is flush with the raw edge on the fabric. Put the overlap in a hidden place, perhaps the center of the back or close to a seam.

- Work your way around the waistband, connecting the anchor points on the elastic with the anchor points on the waistband. The elastic is going to be smaller than the waistband so just keep on pinning around the garment.

- Put the material and elastic into your sewing machine, top edge first, wrong side up. Use a zigzag, overlock, multi-step, or three-step zigzag stitch and make sure the elastic is secured to the fabric and the raw edge is finished at the same time. You can't use a straight stitch for this one.

- As you sew, pull on the elastic and stretch it to make sure it fits the fabric in between each of the anchor points. The stitch you use is going to attach the elastic to the fabric and stop it from moving around while you are wearing the garment. If you opt to use an overlock or serger machine, do make sure the knife on the machine does not cut the material or the elastic.

- Once down, the material should be gathered in, like you see on any elasticated waistband.

- Fold the material and elastic down to the wrong side of the item and pin it in place. Make sure you only fold it down the width of the elastic, ensuring the top of the elastic is at the top of the fabric fold. You will need to stretch both the elastic and the material during this stage because the fabric will have been gathered up to fit the elastic.

- Sew the bottom edge of the fold, wrong side facing upwards, going through the material, stitching, and the elastic. Make sure you stretch the elastic as you are sewing to stop tucks and pinches from being sewn.

- Once you have gone all the way around, the waistband will look as though the elastic has been sewn into a casing but the gathers will be distributed evenly. The elastic will never twist or flip over because it has been secured to your fabric.

10.   Gathering

While the tutorials for gathering may make it look easy, it isn't something you can do with your eyes shut. The sewing is actually the hardest part because you will find your gathers shifting and flattening out, leaving things looking a bit of a mess. Here's how to do it properly:

- Set your sewing machine to the longest length stitch.

- Use a different color of thread in your bobbin just so you know which is which. You will see why when you pull up the gathers.

- Sew a ¼ inch seam allowance in straight stitch.

- Stop about a ¼ inch from the end and drop the needle into your material.

- Raise the presser foot and turn the material to the right, while the needle is in the material.

- Lower the presser foot and take just one stitch.

- Drop the needle down into the material again and raise up the presser foot.

- Turn the material to the right again. You are now ready to sew a parallel line to the first one and the second gathering is going to be 5 mm from the first with a closed end. This will give you a stitch line of ⅜ inch from the edge.

- Sew a line parallel to the first one, making sure there is no crossing over and your lines don't get too close.

- Notice the closed end where you turned the material. This is going to be important for when you pull the threads up to gather the material.

- Lift the needle out of the material, raise the presser foot, and remove the material from the machine. Cut the thread and leave a tail of about seven to eight inches.

- To gather the material up, only pull the bobbin thread. Now you can see why you chose a different color, because it is easier to see. Pull the two bobbin threads carefully, forming gathers that are even. Push the gathers towards the closed end.

This method should give you perfect gathers every single time. Because you closed up the end, you should never be able to pull threads through and lose the gathers. Use a steam iron to press the gathers, ready for ruffling.

Conclusion

I want to thank you for downloading my book; I really hope you found it helpful. I have tried to keep things simple, to explain every step, and to show you though sewing looks difficult and challenging, it really isn't.

Sewing is quickly becoming one of the worlds' most popular crafts again. The rise in the cost of living and the average drop or stagnation of wages means we can't always afford to go out and buy what we want. Whipping up a dress, skirt, or even a t-shirt that looks like it came out of an expensive boutique is not difficult if you concentrate and put your mind to it. As you have seen, it is better to learn how to sew using both a machine and by hand as you can use a combination of the two skills when making your creations.

Once again, thank you for downloading my book. I hope you have lots of fun and produce plenty of unique creations with which to wow your friends and family. Please consider taking a few minutes out of your day to leave a review for me at Amazon.com. Enjoy!

Made in United States
Troutdale, OR
08/23/2023